LOVE IS A LETTER BURNING IN A HIGH WIND

other books by the author
as Daniel Moore

POETRY
Dawn Visions
Burnt Heart/Ode to the War Dead
This Body of Black Light Gone Through the Diamond
The Ramadan Sonnets
The Blind Beekeeper

THEATRE
The Floating Lotus Magic Opera Company
The Walls Are Running Blood
Bliss Apocalypse

COMPILATION OF QUOTES
Warrior Wisdom
The Little Book of Zen
Zen Wisdom (and essay chapters)

as Abd al-Hayy Moore

POETRY
The Desert is the Only Way Out
The Chronicles of Akhira
Halley's Comet
Awake as Never Before

PROSE
Zen Rock Gardening

as Daniel Abdal-Hayy Moore

POETRY
Mars & Beyond
Laughing Buddha Weeping Sufi
Salt Prayers
Ramadan Sonnets (The Ecstatic Exchange revised edition)
Psalms for the Brokenhearted
I Imagine a Lion
Coattails of the Saint
Love is a Letter Burning in a High Wind

PUPPET THEATER
The Mystical Romance of Layla & Majnun

LOVE IS A LETTER BURNING IN A HIGH WIND

poems

September 21 – November 6, 2003

Daniel Abdal-Hayy Moore

The Ecstatic Exchange

2006

Philadelphia

Love is a Letter Burning in a High Wind
Copyright © 2006 Daniel Abdal-Hayy Moore
All rights reserved.
Printed in the United States of America

For quotes any longer than those for critical articles and reviews, contact:
The Ecstatic Exchange,
6470 Morris Park Road, Philadelphia, PA 19151-2403
email: abdalhayy@danielmoorepoetry.com

First Edition
ISBN: 978-0-6151-3599-1 (paper)
Published by *The Ecstatic Exchange*,
6470 Morris Park Road, Philadelphia, PA 19151-240

Cover and text design by Abdallateef Whiteman
www.cwdm.co.uk
Cover collage by the author
Back cover photograph by Malika Moore

On the Road to Konya, and *Rum*i have been previously published in Islamica Magazine.

Dedicated to the teachers and saints
alive now and forever

and to Faruk Dilaver and the soul family in Turkey
and our traveling companions there,
Asmael and Qadirbibi, Mukhtar and Soraya

Gene Gonder, first genius,
Marco Antonio Montes de Oca, first poet,
Sensei Shunryu Suzuki, saintly Zen Master,
Qutb Shaykh Sayyidi Muhammad ibn al-Habib
(*may God be pleased with him*)
—and the living continuation of his teachings—
(Abdal-Qadir as-Sufi, initiator on the Path)
Shaykh Muhammad Rahim Bawa Muhaiyaddeen,
(*may God be pleased with him*)
Baji Tayyaba Khanum, deepest pure devotion,

*The earth is not bereft
of Light*

CONTENTS

1. On the Road to Konya 11
2. Did a Window Go Up? 13
3. Off Rumi's Tomb 14
4. Shams 16
5. Rumi 18
6. Conversation with the Executioner 20
7. Angel Embracing Your Shoulder 23
8. The Dogs of Cappadoccia 26
9. A Rose Appears 27
10. I've Fallen in Love with a Bolt of Lightning 30
11. The Bosphorus 40
12. Little Tiny Drops of Water 42
13. Harp 48
14. Family Portrait 52
15. Creeds 54
16. The Master 55
17. A Story 57
18. The Tale of the Three Cats 63
19. Tulips Line the Walkway 73
20. Every Angle of Our Body 76
21. Sacrifice and Sacrificer 78
22. Anything and Everything Possible 79
23. Tale of the Watermelons 80
24. Golden Waterfall 82
25. Inaugural Address 84
26. A Love Poem 87

27	For One Brief Shining Moment	91
28	Think "*Thrush*" Think *"Bush"*	93
29	Lament of the Ocean	95
30	Others Have Died Before	97
31	Wonder Itself	102
32	Black Cat	104

LOVE IS A LETTER BURNING IN A HIGH WIND

The eye with which I see God
is the very eye with which God sees me.

— MEISTER ECKHART

1   ON THE ROAD TO KONYA

Sometimes I get tired of all this talk about God
and I just want to go and sit under a tree

but then the tree starts talking to me about God
and we find ourselves in another conversation

No two people and no two things talk about God
in quite the same way

A wheel running down a hill all by itself talks about God
while its hub remains stationary and its spokes rotate

An ant has another way of approaching the subject
that has about it a certain collective resonance

Inanimate objects on the other hand often comment on their surroundings
and the pleasant or unpleasant sets of circumstances
that landed them there

Stars have the softest voices and you have to listen more attentively
but their take on the theme is always illuminating
and sheds light in many unexpected and even faraway places

A lover often speaks about God in incomplete sentences
with clouds of various colors and densities
moving slowly or quickly around their
faces and most unselfconscious gestures as they speak in
intimate whispers

And then I'm brought back again to the sweet syrups of this endless
talk about God that goes on every instant
even when no one seems to know what they're talking about
or why they began conversing in the first place

The serpent winks the sunflower opens its concentric
mathematical mandala
flat and desolate wastes yawn and the air shivers

I stick out my tongue and God's breath flows all around it
whether we speak or remain silent as we sail through the
divine events of the sky and earth's decisive

theological arguments with all their perfect proofs and occasional
long and melancholy refutations

9/21
(on the road to Konya)

2   DID A WINDOW GO UP?

Did a window go up and a head lean out to speak?
Has an engine started down on the street at 6:30 in the morning?

Is the world trembling with expectation and excitement?
Are the colors of the world flowing to their designated places?

Has the telephone system of the birds begun ringing each warbling number?
Has light begun squeezing through all the tiniest spaces?

There's a call coming from a very distant location
and everything is trying to listen straining its innermost ears

But it turns out not to be far away at all in this
colossal metropolis of deception that we are
with all our bodily senses

Even a small voice can be projected throughout the entire stadium
and while the lions are chewing on our arms and legs
the spectator in the worst seat can sit up and listen

It's true that the multiple voices of this world can confuse us
but if we listen to their tone and timbre
we hear the song of God's spheres whistling through us
in an uncompromising music of declaration
of the end and beginning of time and space and love and light

and the sweet sigh of the person next to us sleeping

9/21

3 OFF RUMI'S TOMB

Here in the tea hall off the tomb of Mevlana in Konya
there are many different faces but only one beating heart

As we sip brown Turkish tea whose sugar cubes have dissolved
we taste the sweetness of the Unseen in the physical sweetness of the tea

If a flame appeared in the middle of the room
with laughing serpent heads at its
power of consumption of our fragile selves would that
one heart of ours rejoice at last at its union with God?

Our teacher speaks in Turkish with his fingers articulating thought
and great white herons fly from his palm into a dazzling blue sky

At our feet a well of purest water appears and little
golden fish sing in unison about their ardent love of swimming
even if just round and round

They move through the water the way Truth swims through our spirits
parting them invisibly and letting them come together again with no scar
for water and spirit are of a nobler essence than flesh
and one of the great gifts of fluid perfection and purification

The walls are beginning to dance and the floor and ceiling
are already slowly turning as the giant flame shows its holy face

The air is burning but with that flame of God's love that
knows no obstacles and moves as relentlessly as
water toward itself its very intoxicated majestic self
Light upon Light and Face within every face

from the tiny spark of its starting point to the
Paradise-sized flash of its penultimate and ultimate goal

9/21

4   SHAMS

A fiery bear with flashing eyes walks into a parlor
and eats the curtains

A giant chainsaw comes down out of heaven and saws a
house into two perfect halves

A hurricane out of nowhere appears in a crowd
and makes everyone love it to the utmost of passion

Shems appears to the mountaintop of Mevlana
and splits rock to its foundations in Adam's
original earth

Abdal-Hayy's a fraud but hold onto your fraudulence

Abdal-Hayy's empty but hold onto your emptiness

Abdal-Hayy's a worthless cheat but hold onto your
worthlessness

Is there anything more?

Have you anything to defend yourself with?

A tiny shield no bigger than an eyeball?

A shelf of notebooks filled with words?

Good names and reputations are paper sphinxes in
the Egypt of the heart

Shems is executioner but when we push back his
hood it's a full-blooming rosebush full of butterflies

The blood Shems gets on the tip of his sword
is a small price to pay for the alchemical transformation of the
corpse from silver to gold and from
gold to the glory of the Divine Name alone

The threat of death shocks our heartbeats into
higher registers

At the edge of a cliff even a toehold becomes
dubious

In the market of souls Shems slams down a
coin and buys the store

Instead of fleeing merchants bring out their best
wares to add to the pile

At the end of the day he sets fire to it all
and the giant conflagration shouts

Allah!

9/22

5 RUMI

> *Come, come again, whoever, whatever you may be, come;*
> *Heathen, Fire Worshipper, sinful of idolatry, come.*
> *Come even if you have broken your penitence a hundred times;*
> *Ours is not the portal of despair and misery – come!*
>
> — MEVLANA RUMI

The ultimate gorgeous gazelle appears at the edge of our earthly wood
and sniffs the air

The aroma is mixed together from every aroma on earth
and in its delicate nostrils it mingles with the dear scents of heaven

In its pure black eyes is written the Name of Allah
in perfect calligraphic script

Its hooves are shod in gold and its flanks are tasseled
with perfect silver tassels

Its heart is this tomb of yours O Mevlana with your
son Velad behind you and your father Bahauddin in front of you

Its tiny horns glimmer like twin minarets
and its breath which is the breath of God
sounds like the *ney* flute that plays through the air here
endless mournful melodies even sober bumblebees get drunk in

Everyone takes away something of your blessing Mevlana
even the traipsing tourists in shorts with their video cameras
and childlike confusion

The old man with long white beard
who recited from a tattered book counting white
beans by his knees has slowly walked away so bent
over in his black coat but the aroma of his prayer
has stayed behind

Even the echoes are entwining around your words now
and the little child holding her mother's hand
is blinking in time to their eternal rhythm

The gazelle straightens up with dewdrops on its mouth
from grazing in the new morning grass

and leaps away

9/22 (in Rumi's tomb)

6 CONVERSATION WITH THE EXECUTIONER

In a few minutes I will die
and I am happy with the knowledge of my death

whereas you are unhappy not knowing when your
time will come

I have a short time to make my peace with God
and no time left to commit more mistakes
asking forgiveness with every breath

whereas time stretches out before you under
many arches and over many hills with
temptations at every side to taste and err in

I'm filled with joy whose roses bloom with every heartbeat
each second that passes a sweet dispensation
direct from God's hands in giant glorious waves of light

I see with my eyes but I'm blind to this world
which has become a one-way tunnel to my
meeting with my Lord

whereas your sight wanders everywhere
anxious that a sudden blow from behind might
blacken your life
or a fire break out and consume house and
family all the photos and trinkets you've picked up along the way

I've let all these things drift from me one by one
in a great wind that is blowing me
from in front of me whose puckered lips and ballooning
cheeks are from God alone Who's impatient for our
meeting and Who's bringing me to Him in a
special limousine filled with jasmine petals and pages
from His holy books now as translucent as light
and as breathable as air itself

My heart tolls like a bell

My feet and hands tingle with expectation

My body arches forward
whereas yours shrinks back afraid of the
death's head whose grin turns everything to stone

I'm about to be silenced at last with
no more words to trap me

but you have many more *"hellos"* and *"goodbyes"* left
and must take care in every case to fashion sentences that touch
each soul with love rather than hate or hurt

I shall lose this head of mine
and enter the hall of the heart

singing

You shall go home to a silence like the tomb
and make petty conversation

while I sing God's praises with open eyes
and no more blemishes

Here take this shirt to comfort you
and this kiss

Farewell

9/22

7 ANGEL EMBRACING YOUR SHOULDER

Listen

There's an angel embracing your left shoulder with
tears in his eyes

He wants to fly with you but your feet remain
firmly on the ground

There's an angel over your right shoulder whose
wings cover both sun and moon with a
gift for you but your eyes are moving from
side to side so you don't see it

There's an angel standing right in front of you whose
face resembles yours as well as every face God's ever
created on earth in continuous transformation

and he speaks all your sentences and all these
words you write before you write them

and points out a vanishing point on the horizon
where all the conflagrations in the world are
a purifying alembic transfiguring dark riotous

bands of snake power into strands of interstellar
music each of us can sing under our normal
rhythms of breathing

There's an angel in a starry overcoat for each
action and one with an ocean that surrounds
all our hopes to drown in and be saved from
despair each blink of the heart

one in each fingertip to bestow blessings on the
earth instead of curses positive electromagnetic

caresses instead of blows to the head of everything good

There's an angel of dictation just now riding
over the hill in front of me whose
great wings slowly open and close and each time a
new world appears and an old one vanishes

to the neighing of horses and the tiny squeak of
wristwatch wheels those little cogs
that mesh to a whistling tune

Let each angel lunch on the Lord's approval
their only sustenance

for their unearthly substance is a light that
encloses darkness and swallows it

Their breath faces everywhere
appearing again like moons

>					9/23-4
>					(*night of the Miraj – Cappadoccia*)

8   THE DOGS OF CAPPADOCCIA

The dogs of Cappadoccia never stop barking
The muezzins moo like cows

The rocks are shaped like fairy chimneys
from basalt pumice and tuff

The volcanoes that produced them are silent
but the dogs never stop barking

                                                  9/24

9   A ROSE APPEARS

A rose appears and tells me his name is Ahmet
I tell him my name is Ahmet but there is
no confusion

The sentries at the gate salute each other in a
secret hand signal and their eyes' gazes
electrically enter into each other and the
gate opens

Now that it's open I see the place for what it is
Ahmet tells me this

We enter and all the roses start singing at once
each petal making a different kind of music

The air is filled with the sound of chimes

I've never seen so much activity in so much
stillness before
never noticed to much sky in so much earth
never breathed such pure air so free of dust
and the fragrant dust of mortality

A happy lion appears and tells me his name is Ahmet
I tell him my name is Ahmet but there is
no confusion

He shows me the place where all the lions congregate
under the light of a pre-creational sun

I see birds in the shapes of souls wheeling and diving in the
air above a fountain of faces

I leave my cloak behind knowing that if it gets
too cold I'll have a lion for warmth although we must
always be careful with lions and remain on their
good side

The darkness has lifted here and I see we're in a
jungle of heart-shaped leaves and flowers and that they are
entwined flames

It's a white bowl full of flames brought before me by
one of the older lions who gestures with his paw
for me to drink

My name is Ahmet he says
Have no fear

I tip the bowl into my mouth
listening to my heart

I've been instructed to remain silent

We're in a garden
just a regular rose garden

Each rose in the rose garden is named Ahmet
each bird in the sky each particle of dust
each sound in the ears each
heartbeat

I tell them all my name is Ahmet but there is
no confusion

9/25

10 I'VE FALLEN IN LOVE WITH A BOLT OF LIGHTNING

1

I've fallen in love with a bolt of lightning

It comes from far away and leaves nothing untransformed

I've seen horse's heads turn into handsome youths
bouquets of flowers wrap on leafy skirts and
dance under the full moon

I've seen this love commit the most amazing
acts of daring
like walking out on a plank over a precipice
or sitting very still in a crowd of hysterical revelers

It can't be bought at any price
and though it's free the box it comes in is
hard to break open

I've seen whole cities go up in flames at its
mere mention

The slaves lay down their rolling pins and shovels
and take up singing and the laying on of hands

From house to house the same question comes up
"Who are you?" and *"Where are you going?"*

I'm not very clever but I like to
think I am

If the wheel hadn't been invented I'm sure I'd
still be walking

I reach out my hand to catch hold of a rushing train
It takes my hand away and leaves me behind

If you see me anywhere please report me
to the Police

Description: *an open door a crying baby a*

tree on a mountaintop in silhouette a

collection of strange shells incomplete sentences

a letter burning in a high wind

2

A dear friend said to me: *"Take the gold
after it's been dipped in the acid of wisdom"*

Later we discussed alchemy and the ingestion of
transformative drugs
with some credit on my part being given
to the wrenched openings we experienced onto the
next world or the fascinated awareness of the
ongoing metamorphosis of this one

and the alembics and tedious procedures it
took to transform base metals into gold
often leading to cataclysmic explosions

often killing the alchemist

Love is like this

We have these desperately mortal bodies
winding up from babyhood and winding
down from adulthood

But love is the secret of timeless processes

and on the other side is an embrace that
takes place before the creation of worlds

3

The *Buraq* is a beast with a
mule's body and a human head and lightning wings

Its indescribable face more beautiful than
moonlight on lake water or petals on black velvet

And its mule's body is that of a race horse
and its wings are long and stiff like a dragonfly's
and its indescribable face is like that of the
Prophet Muhammad and its eyes are so

pure it's like they've never glanced at
any material thing

and its odor is musk and rose oil
and its noise is wind in ocean coves

and it flew the Prophet to Jerusalem in a few leaps and
bounds as smoothly as if he were rowing

and it spoke to him on the journey of the
things he might be seeing

though it remained silent for the duration
and had no speech to speak of

I can't verify any of this
and it's not meant to be taken as gospel

But the mere contemplation of it excites the heart to
visionary brightness

4

A wasp's nest is not the same as a beehive

I've never figured out what wasps do
but they seem to be mainly interested in stinging

Whereas bees in their peregrinations off in
various directions to whatever sweetness attracts them
seem to be really on a special mission to
survey the territory and gather in the pollen
and turn it into nectar and make
our planet more habitable overall

A snake's mission is to slither away
unless it's lifting its head to strike

venom into our hearts
though there are many gentle second class slenderer snakes who
mind their own business swimming in rivers or raiding
hummingbirds' nests

Danger comes in many disguises and may be
the most glamorous one at the cotillion the most
benign-seeming detractor the most
tempting delight

Our way is clear

Our goal is complete surrender

Our model is how the Creator sends
surrenderers to all the great battlefields and
all races and religions known to mankind
whose love pours from their hair follicles and
fingertips and hearts' incessant praises

extolling the irrefutable One Beloved of us all
the way bees come back to the hive to add their
share to the overall octagonal structure
honoring the central queen and making
medicine for mankind

While wasps build cunning lanterns of brown spit paper under
eaves but are really too
touchy to get close to

and nobody's ever spread wasp nectar on their
toast or had a

spoonful before sleeping

5

Yet love can also have an angry face

And even wasps are running love's errands
nosing around with twitching feelers and leading with their
eyes as best they can

Love's earnestness in these matters is what
matters

To leave snowflakes in the wind is an indication
of love's sheer evanescence

The wind itself is a love pulse and the air itself
love's ubiquitous presence to everyone on earth

needing to inhale however we do and
exhale again in love's continuous rosary
each mite and polar bear witnessing love's
breathing remembrance of reality

If the light gets too intense we
close our eyes
but if we stop breathing we lose our lifeline and dive
down into death
love's close-fitting cloak
love's choker love's single

sleep under so many eyelids

love's sealed envelope sending us to our

true destination

love's passionate kiss around our
entire being

love's personal signature

love's unperplexity

love's light

6

But I'm in love with a lightning bolt
and a laughing heart

Who strings lights from tree to tree and calls it
Christmas

Bathes and dresses in the finest clothes and calls it
'Eid

Wears a Friday shawl and ignites a candle and calls it
Shabbas

Puts gardenias in a golden bowl on the
altar of love in an incense *puja* in the
Himalayas

There's no end to the sea of love in loves' living boat
no rain that doesn't fall from love onto love's rooftops

This lightning bolt has sometimes a human face in half-shadow
except for the eyes

and the eyes loom out of the dark like exuberant song

and ignite every particle of air between where
there is no between

and annihilate any other than itself when there
is no other

for this lightning bolt is a single burst that never ends
whose warm lips touch every heart with a
perfect kiss

It's a dance really from the first breath God's given us
long before our births to the last intake of

breath that takes place long after we're gone

where there is no before nor after no
coming or going no exhalation or intake except

of love's perfection

love's absolutely

perfect perfection

9/26

11 THE BOSPHORUS

I can't stop looking at the Bosphorus
and the black-headed birds that fly by

and the boats that ply the waters back and forth
like earnest children eagerly optimistic

and the vast panorama of clouds like fluffed *Pishmanya* sweets
of spun sugar much beloved by sweet-toothed Turks everywhere

and the red-tiled rooftops with the sound of amplified calls to prayer
back and forth across the city like the eager but serious boats

and Princess Island just offshore with its phallic lighthouse tower
and the doves and black-headed birds landing on the rooftops
to the gurgle of the boat-motors tugs and ferries
even yachts and freighters

on this perfect sunny day in Istanbul the sun on my
back on a terrace on the Asian side and in the

far distance on their monumental promontory
the Haga Sofia and the Blue Mosque with their
electric tower minarets reversing Arthur Rimbaud's

hallucination now in the 21st Century to mean
whenever I look at a mosque I see in its place a factory
which in the original opposite of this is more

comforting to the heart but is sadly 19th Century now

overlooking the Bosphorus on a Friday morning on
September the 26th in the year of our Lord and

Beloved Allah 2003

9/26

12 LITTLE TINY DROPS OF WATER

1

Little tiny drops of water contain the world

I can't see them but I know they're there

A billion angels not only dance on the head of a

pin they carry it through the heavens on the
shoulders of a billion more angels also dancing on
heads of pins carried on a billion more angel

shoulders *ad infinitum* all to an uncanny but
also unreproducible music that may be

Allah's actual breath or the bells and flutes played by
hosts of other angels ranged in orchestras of Light

which I also cannot see but which I
also know are there

along with gardens of Paradise winding through
valleys of a beauty so dazzling one quick tiny blink of squinted
look of our earthly eyes through our
interlaced fingers maybe even behind dark
glasses would make us
swoon a hundred years or more just one

digital flick of our ocular apprehension actually witnessing such a
place for itself might make our hearts burst
out of our chests with its unutterable gorgeousness

so all these things which I can't see all these
whispers of truths and expenditures of credulity

all these things we talk about or avoid
talking about beginning with God's reality or
unreality and going even to our little baby finger
and wondering how it came about to being so
perfect just as it is and especially when either

wiggling freely in the air almost by itself or
able to reach a place in our eyelid to

dislodge an eyelash while we

watch it in a mirror

I mean just look all around and inside us if
you want proofs of these things

one glimpse there also with their

fantastic rainbow bridges arcing across chasms of
scintillating light or canyons of glass with herds of

grazing fabulous animals in them chewing bright

grasses while looking with their deep black innocent eyes

making tiny vapor drops of breath around their
nostrils each one of which contains

a world

2

"Oh it's really not a question of belief or

disbelief cricket children" a grandfatherly figure
bending over nearly double with flowing
white beard and hands on a cane and a
voice of benign sweetness might say one

gentle afternoon by the side of a gurgling river say
or even next to a car dealership in downtown
Istanbul or Philadelphia

It's not really a question of faith or lack of
faith at all because it

all goes on whether or not we

recognize it it spirals into heavens unexpected and un-
presumed it dives down into sea-depths unfathomed

It's so powerfully vast and goes on so
oblivious to our recognizing it or not that all our

arguing and fretting over God's grandeur is really rather
beside the point after all

and especially after death in particular

when we rub our weary eyes weary of so much
lidded sleep and find ourselves there once and
for all and everything we either denied or agreed to
displays itself with the same objective aplomb
the so-called real world did while we
lived in it half or more than half oblivious to

all the miracles that were going on inside and

around us even then with our sharp senses and
razor-sharp intellects doing their best to

keep up with it all when really the best

attack on the whole affair was and is always to just
raise that little pinky finger above that tiny little

drop of water on the linoleum tabletop for once and

see for ourselves the whole situation of how it

happened to get there in the first place and

how our little finger happened to dip in it by

mistake while we were talking or not

talking just that moment with a friend either with or without

long white beard or tears in his eyes recounting the

story of the noble and handsome young son of Prophet Abraham
refusing to be bound for his oncoming sacrifice lest God

think him afraid of his father's knife

that day when belief and disbelief were

tested beyond human endurance

and those dancing angels stopped dancing for a moment to bring down a

live sheep through the seven heavens to replace his son with

and the knife became a blade of water unable to

cut and that water dear children that
fierce blade of separation became the flowing

river of unity connecting us once and for
all with all these wiggling tributaries of human

delving and consequence over the

centuries and millennia when we've all

faced the same old wonderings over and over from the

very dawn of time to its inevitable

sunset and we'll all be faced with it

over and over in our lives *ad infinit*um with each

heartbeat and lung-breath of us

gazing thoughtfully out from one of those

little tiny drops of water out

one of its windows in a drizzly afternoon

contemplating all these consequentially gorgeous and irrefutable

things

13 HARP

1

The harp that is played down the street behind
a wall down some rickety steps past the tombs and
madrasas inside a garden kiosk surrounded with
green and red rosebushes in bloom under a
cloudless sky with only one cloud in the sky above it
in the shape of a benign face with silver beams coming
down from it even finer than rain

is being plucked by invisible hands but the
music it plays is already known by our hearts dear friend

and visible in our eyes when our eyes are gone into the
sky itself whose lids are the aromas the roses give

off with every note of the music

2

The music that is played unheard by all and
known by all has unspoken

words to it equally unheard and
equally known by all so when we

hear those words spoken as if by

miracle by one who's words are not

his or hers but the invisible harpist's we

recognize them in their heart-source as if we'd

been able somehow to say them ourselves which only the

great expunger of selfhood of love can release from our

submerged vocabulary plucked from the deeps there by that

harpist in that kiosk behind that stone fortification which one

step forward evaporates in an instant once that

step forward is also at love's pace and love's

most elegant stride

3

The words to the song the unheard and unspoken

words the hearer hears and the seer sees in the

air as if written there

Oh Allah no words of ours can sing it true

but Yours no melody can catch exactly the

pure song we'd really like to sing but silence

silence Your special note that surrounds all the

other notes Your special space that surrounds all the

stars and planets just as it surrounds each

heartbeat of ours isn't the song itself but the

introduction of the singer to the ever-present assembly of angels

on every leaf and every grass blade

and the concluding stampede of space and time forward again

once the song is done

4

Harpist play that song again don't let it lag

Heartbeat hear its tone as it plucks us home

Notes like phoenixes rising in fire to the Source of Fire

Bring us closer with every beat to Your bending Face

Silence is all and song is all so let us know them
each by Your perfect breath

I can't know You without knowing You nor
hear You without hearing You

There in Your Hiddenness and Here in Your Presence

My heart is Your harp each string of it Yours

Your fingertips touch them and make them ring

Invisible harpist closer than our souls

Refusing to hear You is only for fools

9/27

14 FAMILY PORTRAIT

My daughter wears a million butterfly wings

Where does she wear them and why does she wear them
I don't know

One son wears a bow and arrow above his head
with the Prophet's name on it
because his only desire is to aim true and reach the
central eye

The other son wears flying shoes made especially for him
exclusively with no manufacturer's mark on them anywhere

My wife wears a heart where a heart should be
and her own heart approaches it with every
passing moment with the names of all the
prophets inscribed on it and all the
Names of Allah

I wear butterfly wings bow shoes and her heart inside my heart

and as the butterfly wings open so do I open

and as the bow is drawn I tremble

and as the shoes fly my road becomes shorter

and with each heartbeat of hers we
approach the Garden as our first parents did

with sweet humility

9/27

15 CREEDS

If divorce is the only way divorce with civility

If despair is the only way despair with dignity

If fear is the only way fear with humility

If censure is the only way censure with humanity

If judgment is the only way judge with temerity

If desire is the only way desire with frugality

If ambition is the only way be ambitious with integrity

If reason is the only way reason with spontaneity

If love is the only way love with totality

If travel is the only way travel with variety

If submission is the only way submit with alacrity

If love of God is the only way love God with consistency

If arrival is the only way arrive with ecstasy

9/27

16 THE MASTER

The Master lays down his bow and arrows
and sends the point home with a quick

flick of his eyelids

A tree moaned in the Prophet's mosque because he
neglected to lean on it when he spoke

Locomotive wheels go faster than the eye can see
but in their place they're stationary at their
designated rotation

Everything is always so much more than we can imagine
I'm always amazed at how little amazement at
all things we feel

unless I'm mistaken

Dolphins leap before the prow of a boat
smarter than we think

Whales in the pale blue depths of the sea when the
sunlight penetrates it move like
unsinkable Titanics with God alone their impeccable captain

The Master knows all this and never stops
diving and bringing the depths themselves

up to our surfaces

O Face of the one I love through all its
permutations

I can't stop drinking from your features since they're
the expression of your soul

and your eyes which are unpredictable
oceans reading the thoughts of everyone and

everything from right to left and from
left to right

as if balancing our heart-ventricles with the
scanning of your pupils

twin lenses of God's single Light!

9/27

17 A STORY

1

I want to tell a story from out of the
great golden ball of stories

perhaps with talking or thinking animals such as the
rhinoceros in the veldt who wishes it were a

slender white stork rather than a battleship gray
thick-skinned squinty-eyed rhino I mean it

watched the graceful stork from its side of the
high pampas grasses but could only lumber

forward at admittedly often rapid speeds when impelled but could
never just take off into the blue sky a white wide
bird-wing'd flyer through clouds and sunlight

So the rhino grew glum a bit and stewed in its *rhinoness*
until one day and here's where we need a

parable of some kind an epiphany in which a
large slow generally blind creature saves the

day or does what only a rhino can do to free a
lion perhaps from a trap or in a burst of light

turns into a hunky prince after all or even
better becomes a rhino totally

satisfied with its lot in life in the perfect rhinoceros
slot God selected for it in the wide world of

possibility on the one hand and limitation on the
other where the sun could only be a

burning ball of violently erupting gases and not say a
reflective moon or a silken lily growing from a secret sweet lagoon

and though we can always dance out in perfect
stillness past our body's limits into planetary

motions and paradisiacal effervescent flowering we come
back to *"pass the salt please"* and *"excuse me"*
in crowded elevators and *"I guess this is goodbye"* in quiet hospitals

But the rhino wept a little through his
squinty eyes to see the stork so freely flying

and his heart opened to the stork next time it
landed near him and they entered into

deep intimate conversation about each other's lot

and it turned out the stork envied the rhino often too

its sheer weight and solidity and its lovely charcoal
iron-plated skin instead of feathers needing constant preening

and uncertain skies to fly in and unexpected predators

2

So there's the stork's story and the rhino's story
as well as the beetle's through the pampas grasses

who came all this way to trudge up blades and down
stalks to hear them chatting and he was

immediately struck with the relevance to himself
having perhaps read Kafka and having to live his

whole life taunted for being a beetle though he
often points out the translation from the

German might better be *"cockroach"* or *"vermin"*

Still he overheard them comparing envies and thought of all the
envies he feels in a day and yet seen from

above perhaps it would seem to be just a moseying
beetle minding its own business rather than a

sentient creature deeply affected by an overheard conversation
and its heart opening to a new possibility of not

reacting enviously but seeing itself in a beetle pattern as well as
a divine one and able to fuse the two into a

feasible whole

3

But when we mention the rocks and trees and grasses themselves
we may get yet another matter and altogether
more vibrant or less eventful stories though I

can't imagine the patience it would take to
listen all the way through to the punch line of a
rock's story or the riddle a patch of sky might

propose or the guessing-game of grasses with all the
fluttering competition between grass blades to be the first to answer

though the sky's unraveling tale might be truly
fascinating since it has seen in its day the *dance macabre*
as well as the celebratory *shodishes* of history

the mass movements the taking to streets the entire village with
torches in their hands on a winter's night as well as the

poignant doings perhaps in a windy garret with one
coughing match girl and her orphan or rather too-soon-to-be

orphaned child who grows up in the

severest hardship and in various foreign countries
at the hands of sometimes beneficent sometimes sadistic
doctors and lawyers

But then one day in his teens he goes away to
college somehow through the grace of a Dickensian
benefactor perhaps and studies what he's
always been interested in which takes us a
few years later to his explorations in Africa

on tiptoe to get nearer to our stork and our

rhinoceros not to shoot them or at least not
lethally since they now grace the cover in full color of

The National Geographic although the picture's caption
doesn't mention anything of their

conversation and nothing of its subject of envy and humble acceptance
since the photographer anthropologist is so
pleased to get the shot and happily

envies no one at all but is completely satisfied
with God's wriggly plan all along as it has

opened layer after layer not necessarily to his
perceptions but to his

viscerally existential sense of his khaki-clad self as he

caps the lens of his camera and tiptoes away
and the stork remarks to the rhino

*"I hope you were smiling since that
chap in the pith helmet over there just took your
snapshot they do it all the time now and I
didn't have a chance to sail over a
body of water first to make sure all my plumage was in place"*

and the rhino replies

*"God's placed each of your feathers perfectly
you look absolutely great my dear –*

how do I look?"

10/1

18 THE TALE OF THE THREE CATS

for Afnan Blankinship

I

There were three cats who lived at the bottom of a
well

a big desert well you can walk down steps cut in the
wall so there's lots of room for three cats to pounce and sleep
and though not the most commodious and
wide-open living space at least they were
never far from water and small mice

A rich merchant took a fancy to one of them one
day and his servants coaxed it and caught it and they
popped him in a camel bag and took him to
Baghdad

He lived in luxury coming and going in the tiled
corridors and sumptuous halls running his claws down
available brocades and sleeping on silk
pillows among curling wafts of incense

Have I told the story of the second cat yet?

No

A poor man climbed painfully down the
steps to the well below about as
poor as you can get without turning completely inside-out
and fell in love with the second cat so he
coaxed it and caught it and put it in his wide empty *djallaba* pocket and
trudged up the earthen steps and hobbled onto his

lank donkey and they toddled off across the
desert to his hovel in a small village where he
gathered firewood and sold it at the
tag end of the market among the rusted key stalls and
merchants of busted iron pipes and bent nails and the cat
followed him into the woods and caught mice
and followed him home again where he
slept on a greasy turban in a shabby corner
happy whenever sunlight landed on him from the
many gaping roof-chinks

The third cat in this feline trilogy is a bit
harder to figure

We could leave him there though lonely and he could
as it were hold the fort for the inevitable
return of the other two
or he could get eaten by one of those
pointy-eared desert foxes which would alas
dispense with one plot twist at least

or he could miraculously transform one early
morning into a stunningly handsome desert boy and climb
out of that well into a kind of victorious Joseph in
Egypt dispensing sheaves of wheat and Godly justice

but that might throw the story off so let's just
leave the third cat for the moment sleeping on the
tenth step in oblivious peace

Well one day a moose walks into the pasha's palace
I have no control over these things
maybe it was a gift from the Ambassador to Canada
a not too huge moose perhaps only a young moose calf
with nevertheless very large antlers and a sunny disposition

The cat awoke and its hairs all three million seven hundred and
twelve of them stood out straight to the
musical accompaniment of servants' screams the
clatter of tea-trays the crashing of valuable
china the high squeals of eunuchs rushing in
all directions with quick shuffling motions in fact

everyone in the palace except the ladies of the harem
who saw in this exquisitely ungainly beast a

bit of diversion from their easy but tediously same same
existence

They rushed up to the moose though cautiously when nearest
and calmed its fears and looked into its
wild eyes

They gently led it by its mane and chin-hairs to their
quarters

The cat was appalled but curious and stood on
cat tiptoe on its silken cushion to see the
women in their chiffon and jewelry leading a

moose into the lap of luxury

2

I've been very tempted to
scuttle this poem altogether as a result of getting myself
hopelessly cornered having introduced a
moose to divert attention from the
first story but for three days now unable to

come up with anything for the second which is
nevertheless easier and more

straightforward he being a poor man and the
cat being content with little but a few thin

threads of sunlight and a mouse or two
its early days in the well accustoming it to
privation and delight in the play of

dust in the air or a few pebbles on the ground

whereas our first cat who soon became a
fat cat in every way lounged and lazed in luxury and
rubbed its muzzle on gold snuff boxes and
lacquered trays

now faced with a moose maybe more fictional than real
though the harem women found him handsome
decorating his antlers with woven macramé and jewels and
brushing his moosey body glossy

Our first cat recalling his early years with a
shudder as he scratched his neck avoiding the
diamond choker and dreaming of pillows piled even
higher in a sunlit glade where mice are
served in style with little paper
booties and a side of caviar

3

The one remaining cat of the three the one still
living in the well closes his eyes and finds himself
everywhere

He's stayed close to the Source so he really
doesn't need to go anywhere

Drinkers come down the steps parched after days in
hot exposure and drink like thirsty camels

They see him almost as an Egyptian icon either
sitting full height with slitted eyes closed
or sleeping head on paws and tail curled
tightly around his slim black body

and pass on

High and low are the same to him his luxury

to never stray from the depth in dryness the
water from the center of the earth he listens to both
day and night
whatever moon-phase bejewels the well-walls at whatever
day of the month or year or whatever
millennium happens to pass over him

though I don't mean to imply that this slightly tattered
lean and furry specimen is immortal in its flesh and fur

yet he's *felinical* fidelity itself each purr of which
reaffirms the Creator of whiskers and claws
rather than whiskers and claws themselves
the Sovereign over wet and dry and the
God of the flung nets of starlight in the night sky
he watches above him through the porthole well-shaft cut there
in the earth like a telescope of Galileic wisdom
with a direct view of sun and moon Venus and mars
Aldebaran and The Pleiades

4

Why a moose? What purpose does its bizarre appearance serve?

Our first cat has befriended the Eeyore-looking one
and sometimes curls up on his antler's rack to sleep
companionable to the other beast allowed in the
sumptuous human camp other than the occasional
tiger that leaps out of the night to drag away a
screaming slave or baby but this only on a
rare occasion igniting legend decades later

But then one day earth's mortal fortunes change and a devastation
flattens the palace and guts the royal treasure and everyone
flees in all directions and only the moose and cat remain
looking out through
ruined arches and burnt gardens blasted trees past
dry fountains and stubble

"Well" the cat says finally to leaning friend moose
"I must be going"

Moose replies *"Me too – I'm going with you!"*

So cat on antler crow's nest and slowly plodding moose head out for
home at least the
cat's origin since the moose would have to book a
flight for Ontario or even further north and
we have to assume airplanes haven't been
invented yet but don't ask me how it
got there in the first place

The second cat's owner also had a reversal
and married into a wealthy family whose
happy daughter attracted to her new husband's
resourcefulness and brooding good looks was also unfortunately
allergic to cats so he put his beloved
cat no less beloved than his wife but needing her love
back a bit more than his on his now fat donkey and they
rode off in the morning to the well where our
cats were first found

5

It's high time to bring this saga to an end

Yet I can picture their meeting a little before
dusk moose and cat man on donkey and cat
rendezvousing by the side of the well and our

well-keeper cat opening its deep topaz eyes to the

sweet spectacle of their destined return

There's mewing and sniffing and rubbing of faces and
twitching of tails and long conversations in cat
silence in the night that very

mysterious way cats have of talking to each other that
seems to us at times as deep indifference
and the moose stands by the well-mouth and
meets with camels and horses amazed at the
sight and happy to know of a very different
kind of hoofed animal and of their
early youth in desert wastes and the woody wilds of North America

And the cats recognize our third cat as their
elder and master and learn from it by simple but
detailed courtesies

And they end their days as they began them
on the carved earthen steps of the well

listening to the water that never ends
and to the mice that mistakenly think
the coast is clear

for they're cats first and last

from tip to tail

and from front to rear

10/7

19 TULIPS LINE THE WALKWAY

Tulips line the walkway interspersed with roses

Blue flames in cups of interstellar honey or red flames
in stationary pinwheels

Why is it flowers are all emblems of something in the
Unseen?

They grow up from seeds into free air
proceeding from dark into light

Flowers in the shapes of disasters at sea

Flowers like stairways down which rich
potentates or debutantes might come dressed in their
best

Or poor pale flowers in shapes of characters from Dickens
begging by their poverty or singleness of beauty
to augment the clear but simple designation of their
humble forms

OK there are none really shaped like stairways or
runaway locomotives

But still they all seem to stand for something
rare and fragile a love gift to us from a divine
quite near admirer or some
sweet seducer anxious to win our hearts by plying us with
beauty

Tulips and roses lining our strides forward our
impetuous eagerness even our vain
foolishness

Or when tragedy strikes they're given to us in floral
bunches and bouquets like warm greetings from the
unseen toward which the victim is blowing now like
spiritual pollen

But horseshoes of flowers are also draped around
victorious racehorse's necks for their proud
walk into the Winner's Circle

Petal by petal God's lips form each one like
glass blowers fashioning each nuance into created perfection

Flowers both the calling cards and the goal
the stepping-off point from our origin and
Paradise itself

and the tiny bright rainbowy cheering sections of our
lugubrious progress toward Paradise again

where tulips from the Unseen line our difficult walkway
interspersed with Ecstasy's roses

                                                                   10/9

20 EVERY ANGLE OF OUR BODY

Every angle of our body is a
scroll laid out in heaven and read by angels

Every knee-flex elbow-bend or turn of torso
makes waves of light and heat reverberate as
far as Neptune

Eye-rolls and tongue-lolls and insouciant
tosses of the head or lurchings forward

have somewhere trumpets blown in celestial fanfare
influencing the outcome of a race of

fireflies to the finish line of night's deepest
darkness

Our actual situation in space the actual
longitude and latitude we assume at any given
time makes meridian lines curve in shooting
arcs across geographical projections even

out over oceans where choruses of terns and
an occasional albatross congregate to form in flight
a similar shape in the air

A flick of the finger an eyelid twitch O God

all echoed in Your resonant heaven or rather

our attitudes and earth-gyrations are echoes of

previous but simultaneous actions in pre-creation
in Your sphere by Your sweet inflection
whose ligaments between act and shadow are

love's breath-webs woven with strong but
delicate finesse

                                                            10/10

21 SACRIFICE AND SACRIFICER

A shoe fits the hearer sooner than the message
penetrates the hearer's heart

A dust mote flies through the air at
supersonic speeds
unseen by most but felt across the world

You've heard everything a hundred times so
what's the point?

One sheep of self slaughtered on the altar of the heart
liberates the rest of us bound hand and foot with

lack love given or received until the
instant the knife of separation fails to cut

and sacrifice and sacrificer are set free

10/11

22 ANYTHING AND EVERYTHING POSSIBLE

The heat from the full moon curls up the curtains
on the windows like hair

Love I'll say anything now that you've
got me in your clutches and are
paying the bills

A clown with a flame where his heart used to be
dances patterns of his delirium in the snow

You can't read them but they'll never melt
and in their place Birds of Paradise will grow

Anything is possible and does

Everything is possible and is

              10/12

23 TALE OF THE WATERMELONS

A greengrocer admired the sizes of his watermelons
but failed to notice the severed heads among them
from a battle that hadn't even taken place
over real estate that both sides thought was theirs

A wandering dervish walked by in patched robe with
crooked staff and looked them over in their bin and said to them

"Now see what you've gone and done you poor misguided souls
when a few cups of tea and some pure and
fearless generosity could have solved the case!"

The customers snickered and nudged each other and
pointed the dervish out and the greengrocer laughed

"Nothing belongs to us in the first place you unfortunate men
no use fighting over what belongs to God"
he continued but to the townspeople a
madman was talking to watermelons nothing more

A year later the market was burned to the
ground and in its place a
battlefield arose on whose bloodied soil
many severed heads lay with anguished
expressions on their faces as if beseeching the
God of Mercy on their behalf as they had been
cut in half and their seeds spewed on the ground

The greengrocer sought out the dervish and
gave him his head as well as his
heart and soul so that he'd be

more acceptable to the market of the Next World
than to this

and now he wanders from town to town
leaving some townspeople bewildered some enraged but
most of them thumping watermelons or
severed heads equally without realizing it

in a soporific sleep so deep often only a
quick blade to the neck region or a

crawling labyrinthine binding vine is the only way
to liberation

10/14

24 GOLDEN WATERFALL

A golden waterfall high on a hill
and those suddenly unfurled ferns
as big as houses

Stones of greater girth than the Grand Canyon
lying on its side in full sun just
scattered as if tossed into place some sinking
up to their nonexistent necks
and turning their faceless countenances
to the wind
that blows in huge imageless sheets
from far away whose head start gives it
accelerated rumble as of giants vigorously sweeping
or weeping or raising their voices one by one
bellowing equally over everything with
gale force toward a single distant point way off

and into this scene drift faces like lidded moons or clouds
as if to announce a pending cataclysm or paradigm shift
or float across only to remind us of the recently
dead or the recently being born across
rubble and shale

where a rabbit footprint appears and a
few black beetles clacketing up and down

and a voice enters not quite lamenting and
not quite alerting

and the air falls equally everywhere at once
filled with cavernous ozone

temples of breathable song

10/16

25 INAUGURAL ADDRESS

The inaugural address of the deaf-mute took under
five minutes followed by a general celebration that included
gas-balloon rides and dancing on the head of a pin

If this world were run by saints instead of sinners
we'd probably have to get up to something else to cause
mortal friction

The waterslides for the water buffalo lead them into
almost impossible swamps but their
general good nature prevailed and they
picked themselves up and ruminated thoughtfully for a
full hour before moving again

Women and men eyed each other with suspicion as is
the generic or *genderic* custom then threw
all caution to the winds as usual and settled down to
lives of quiet and unquiet desperation to a
strict yearly schedule of raucous holidays and occasional
civil wars

The elephants at the Inaugural a year before remembered to the
precise detail and tapped on the doors of the
wisest among us which were usually great

grandmothers but also a bent-over plumber and three
tap dancing instructors and they
convened on a Saturday and came up with a
new social code by Monday in which

seeing is believing and believing is seeing

*Respect is due to all and none are
exempt from according just measure*

One monk who'd been in isolation for over ten
years turned out to be a social progressive
remembering the mentally and culturally
challenged as well as the rights of
birds and squirrels

If saints took this world by the lying forelock and
gave it a shake would the
annoyances and injustices slide off the
natural inclination of the planet's rotation and join other
stellar debris in free space?

Or would even goodness soon seem to be suspect?
An age-old question

Often while the worst wars are in full swing
someone is planting bean rows learning a foreign language or
carving a workable sewing machine out of wood

After the speech the deaf and dumb president
had his cabinet of three blind men two
eloquent librarians an animal trainer and
the rest a variety of professions including
naturally a poet and a modern composer as well as a
highwire aerialist and an African dentist
convene on a high mountain for a day of either
meditation or contemplation depending on their natural
inclination and then without a word each went back

to their constituents empty-handed to begin labors of
love on every street and avenue that meant
tree-planting rock-moving and piano-playing
or the taking up periodically of a
variety of instruments in street-corner combos
in praise of the One Invincible and Invisible over all and

with none in any greater proportion than
another though one sing and another count
in full moon or full sunlight

until both macaque and macaw come home again

in furred and plumaged peace and dignity

10/19

26 A LOVE POEM

A love poem circulates among the guests
and makes them all drunk

Goes up one wall and down the next with its
radical interior makeover

Takes everyone outside to dance like nymphs
along a thin silver river until they reach the sea

A love poem doesn't call long distance from a payphone
but opens up inside us with an
oddly familiar melody somehow in harmony
with the sound of thunder and the
tiny whistle of a single sunflower growing

A love poem went out without a name one day and
came back with everyone's name pinned on its shirt
as in a major religious ceremony
where relics that belonged to every
saint ever alive are carried in a solemn procession
tiny knucklebones and eyelashes in glass vials lovingly preserved

This is not only a love poem between two souls in their
urge to become one
it's also between a leaf and the air it grows in
a sound and the simultaneous echo it makes by speaking forth

Arriving just in time is the key to hearing it
like someone walking into the downrush of a waterfall
interrupting the downfall with the ecstatic
rush of cold water on flesh

All the creatures in the surrounding woods
resound with its joy
ants halt for a moment to listen then twitch the
news of it along through their antennas

An eagle knows the domain it surveys is blessed
as it circles and dives

One whisper of a love poem to another is enough to set
avalanches in motion
not arriving at their gravitational destination until the last person standing
gets weak in the knees and starts turning in constellational circles
gazing at the moon

Sleek horses hear it in their stalls and become restless
sleeping hearts hear it in their chests and yearn to fly

It gilds every landscape for miles around with glittering delicate outlines
and cuts through canyons with an ice floe's gargantuan authority

But on the lips of a lover it's enough to attract bees from
China merchants of rare silks from
Samarqand butterflies from Brazil
or the seismic trembling of the hardest heart of a tyrant
even though no tears may come

Between a bride and a bridegroom it's a secret code
known only to them
in a language known by all

It's an unfamiliar garden full of unpronounceable blooms
and a sensation so common you almost
flick it away from your face

It's the air-ocean we swim in just by being alive
and every sound we hear in the world is its ardent articulation

Mortal greetings and final farewells are its middle stanzas
sighs and wide eyes are its opening lines and
bright babbling its closing ones like
water rushing over pebbles or rain on a windowsill

We look out through love's windows onto love's
windows looking back at us
and between are love's walls that are
no walls at all

but God's transparencies He's put everywhere to read
His Names and Attributes in through the
grammar of matter and matter's
ultimate dissolution

at which point love enters us as naked as light
and bathes itself from head to toe
in our simple splendor

10/21

27 FOR ONE BRIEF SHINING MOMENT

In Memoriam Hajj Abd al-'Aziz Redpath

For one brief shining moment
the picket fence bursts into flame that encloses
the dream house

the dream house conflagrates that encloses the
sleeping dreamers

and you awake in time to say that one true thing at the last
as the earth turns a full click on its axis

And somewhere a steaming cappuccino is being
served in your honor
a conversation is being struck up with a total
stranger the way you did
a last penny is being given to a filthy
beggar the way you would

And waves of oceans on all seven wind their
eternal clocks tighter and then
release white froth on silent beaches
and exotic birds flash brilliant plumage and
disappear the way you appeared among us

singing off-key but with deep earnestness
and now are silent so that the
sea waves may cross over into silence to where
you might be

forwarding address unknown

at peace in all your

unearthly restlessness

                                                                10/24

28 THINK "THRUSH" THINK "BUSH"

Think *"thrush"* think *"bush"* think
a basket full of flaming hearts
everyone on earth tries to claim and redeem
torn from their chests in an excess of wonder or
wonderment at shafts of light coming
straight down from God onto this earth's
pockmarked skin at all hours of day or night

unseen except by God's eyes within the eyes of everyone

Think nothing at all or think suddenly of nothing
and then waters rise and flood us with a
new way of seeing
waters of a finer substance waters with no
sleep in them but also tiny flying fish with
human faces going upstream to spawn
when *"upstream"* means into the Glorious Unseen
realms of purest movement and stillness
not beyond this tactile touch that encases us
but within it and surrounding it

Think *"subterfuge"* or our usual maneuvers to somehow
avoid the outrush and onrush

Think nothing at all then think nothing beyond that

A Face fills us with delight

God's Face alone what fills us

10/25

29 LAMENT OF THE OCEAN

One day the ocean said to its Lord
"O Lord I have so many wrecks inside me
I've swallowed so many souls shouldn't I show some
remorse or responsibility at least for all the
lives I've taken?

Bowsprits rest on my sea bottom boxes of ammunition
rusted cannon and shattered amphorae scattered on my sea floor
whole ships serious sharks swim through and
industrious barnacles colonize
personal effects belt buckles shoe-buttons watches eyeglasses
though few bones and few skeletal remains

All of this in my deepest bowels while
giant fish schools swim by in flashing sheets and my waves shuttle across
indifferently and my frothing surf beats shores
as rhythmically as before waves pulled out of themselves by the moon

All shores I slosh as rhythmically and indifferently as the
rotation of the earth with all its living and its
dead tucked deep inside it all Your wide spaces
expanding throughout themselves

*Shouldn't I at least
show some indication of my awareness other than
to You alone?"*

But the ocean went on pouring itself out of itself and
drawing itself into itself again under
both sun and moon as always

Though the sky might have smiled above it for a
moment

The sky might have paused above it for a moment to look down
through its waters to where its wrecks lay scattered on the sea floor
and put a watery hand on broken prows and shattered
caskets

And lovingly counted each tooth and finger bone one by one
as octopus jelly fish
blue whales or schools of electric stingrays
scuttle by

                                                                     10/29

30 OTHERS HAVE DIED BEFORE

1

Others have died before and others will
die after us and yet it's

always a surprise

Water balloons burst on pointed pickets and
splatter the grass

In the empty house tumblers fill with dust

Carcasses of bugs everywhere shell casings whose
crawling food-seekers have either
gone of God's volition in the scheme of things
or been sucked out by ants

It's Autumn in Philadelphia and the yellow leaves are like
a gilder's been so busy gilding them the entire
forest glitters gold in the chill sunlight

When we say goodbye to anyone they may be taken away
by a dark beastly herd and never seen again or
be heard again only in voice or be seen again only in face
and so begin to fragment and dissolve

The forward parade never ends great aunts grandmothers
eccentric uncles with toupees only glimpsed once or
twice at holiday gatherings now only in a brown
photograph when courting his wife of sixty years

Kings on horses at the heads of armies then
drawn by horses in hearses at an army's
rear

Letters in scrawl or perfect handwriting left in a drawer
under handkerchiefs

How did we know we were ever alive?

Though hearsay? How
can we be sure? Is the oasis

far ahead?

2

You don't want to look into the eyes of the dead
that should be seeing but are dead
which is why we close the lids of the dead
wondering why we're alive and making us wonder
why they are dead

Glazed eyes with no life in them that only
moments before were alive

The living soul's been taken away like a
light from a window leaving only the
dull glass instead which is why we respectfully
touch closed the eyelids of the dead

For they might see us from their side we might
know that they see us from this side of life
and uncannily catch us in a net they themselves don't
devise for us but from that
dimension of death that white ocean that
totally sonorous echo on a chord of voices so
vast all other sounds including the free scrape of
planets in their annual orbits are swallowed in it
and swallow us as well by a kind of
acknowledged superiority of the death state or the

assumed but false finality of all our states in death
looking at us directly for the first time now through
eyes that are suddenly dead and without life

O God
bless them and us on
both sides!

3

Running by the side of a freight train full blast as
fast as feet can carry us

Standing as tall as we can in a room with low
ceiling uneven floor and no chairs

Sitting in a green meadow hoping for lightning or at
least the appearance of cows

Counting the bright ribbons in her hair braided in those
twists glistening ebony black

All these lively and alive things our right cheeks on a pane of
cold glass that runs parallel along our lives at
all times

through which we see ourselves identical to
ourselves doing everything we do at the same time

Yet somehow there's a mythic element an element of
misty dark waters opening onto a deathly sea
grinning Charon and his barge slowly poling it
or skies that open to radiance music and tall
stairways in an upward spiral
inconceivable really in any detail but eternally fascinating to our
minds hungry for imagined vistas and savored feasts

each savor curled within the tasteless
each vista tucked inside a blind man's lids

each word dangling on the fragile hook that
swings just out of reach or earshot in our
daily existence

Elusiveness somehow built into our beings so that we
don't rely on ourselves or others alone
nor have total confidence in this doorway or
that rock this plank or that elevator

but turn with burning eyes and hearts on fire
to the one quenching water that flows between
all things and whose substance is His whispered Name

God always above and below and always

before and after

all

10/29-30

31 WONDER ITSELF

The fish in the ocean who's thirsty not somehow
appreciating its immediate situation

The bird in flight who feels hemmed in not even
noticing it's flying already and so will have to
fly out of itself in full splendor to assure itself that
air's whistling past it at high speed because it's
aloft in it not because it's windy

In this membrane of existence itself for want of a
better name full of atoms and gnats and glimmering fireflies
wishing to be totally in touch and torches of
fiery life in full blaze aware of the
Divine Presence face to face if that's our theology

Or wisps and whiskers of the Void on us as close to us
as our flesh is
as intimately part of us as the words out of our mouths

We hold our hands in front of our faces and feel separate from life
move in space from A to B and panic that
life is passing us by or passing too quickly

Think one thought after the other and lament that
nothing proves to us the existence of the action of The Living One
as if we needed to fall down stairs to experience
loss of control or submission to the
gravity of the Goal

Drinking water through a straw when an ocean
utterly surrounds us and breathes us in as

lovingly in fact as we breathe it in and as

deeply and satisfyingly and breathes us
out again

completely until there's nothing left of us to
wonder but Wonder itself

11/6

32 BLACK CAT

I have a black cat who looks fantastic against
the dark red quilted coverlet on the bed
and who purrs extremely loudly when it's spread
and takes up her compactly reclining stance at the
foot of the bed her sphinx-like posture on her
haunches and elbows with paws curled under and does that
very cat-like squinting of eyes while energetically
motoring inside with a vocable in-and-out
on-rolling purr and looks around slowly or
positions her face in intentional profile with triangular ears
cocked and waits for nothing expectantly amidst
a vast red sea upon which she's the
lone phantom schooner as black and as
glossy as a starry night even now audibly
content or proprietary or just being very much a
cat feeling or thinking whatever it is a
cat feels or thinks in its pure sensation of perfectly centered
catness in the dark solar core of her perfectly furred and
satisfied universe
as I write this

11/6

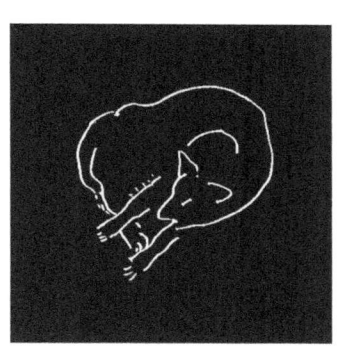

ABOUT THE AUTHOR

Born in 1940 in Oakland, California, Daniel Abdal-Hayy Moore's first book of poems, *Dawn Visions*, was published by Lawrence Ferlinghetti of City Lights Books, San Francisco, in 1964, and the second in 1972, *Burnt Heart/Ode to the War Dead*. He created and directed *The Floating Lotus Magic Opera Company* in Berkeley, California in the late 60s, and presented two major productions, *The Walls Are Running Blood*, and *Bliss Apocalypse*. He became a Sufi Muslim in 1970, performed the Hajj in 1972, and lived and traveled throughout Morocco, Spain, Algeria and Nigeria, landing in California and publishing *The Desert is the Only Way Out*, and *Chronicles of Akhira* in the early 80s (Zilzal Press). Residing in Philadelphia since 1990, in 1996 he published *The Ramadan Sonnets* (Jusoor/City Lights), and in 2002, *The Blind Beekeeper* (Jusoor/Syracuse University Press). He has been the major editor for a number of works, including *The Burdah* of Shaykh Busiri, translated by Shaykh Hamza Yusuf, and the poetry of Palestinian poet, Mahmoud Darwish, translated by Munir Akash. He is also widely published on the worldwide web: *The American Muslim*, DeenPort, and his own website, among others: www.danielmoorepoetry.com. The Ecstatic Exchange Series is bringing out the extensive body of his works of poetry, beginning in 2005 with *Mars & Beyond, Laughing Buddha Weeping Sufi, Salt Prayers* and a revised edition of *Ramadan Sonnets*, and continuing in 2006 beginning with *Psalms for the Brokenhearted, I Imagine a Lion, Coattails of the Saint, Love is a Letter Burning in a High Wind*, and *The Flame of Transformation Turns to Light*. *Abdallah Jones and the Disappearing-Dust Caper* is the tenth in the series, and the first for young adults in the Ecstatic Exchange / Crescent Series.

POETIC WORKS BY DANIEL ABDAL-HAYY MOORE

Published and Unpublished
(many to appear in *The Ecstatic Exchange* Series)

Dawn Visions (published by City Lights, 1964)
Burnt Heart/Ode to the War Dead (published by City Lights, 1972)
This Body of Black Light Gone Through the Diamond (printed by Fred Stone, Cambridge, Mass, 1965)
On The Streets at Night Alone (1965?)
All Hail the Surgical Lamp (1967)
States of Amazement (1970)

The Chronicles of Akhira (1981) (published by Zilzal Press with Typoglyphs by Karl Kempton, 1986)
Mouloud (1984) (A Zilzal Press chapbook, 1995)
Man is the Crown of Creation (1984)
The Look of the Lion (The Parabolas of Sight) (1984)
The Desert is the Only Way Out (completed 4/21/84) (Zilzal Press chapbook, 1985)
Atomic Dance (1984) (am here books, 1988)
Outlandish Tales (1984)
Awake as Never Before (12/26/84) (Zilzal Press chapbook, 1993)
Glorious Intervals (1/1/85) (Zilzal Press chapbook, ?)
Long Days on Earth/Book I (1/28 – 8/30/85)
Long Days on Earth/Book II (Hayy Ibn Yaqzan)
Long Days on Earth/Book III (1/22/86)
Long Days on Earth/Book IV (1986)
The Ramadan Sonnets (Long Days on Earth/Book V) (5/9 – 6/11/86) (Published by Jusoor/City Lights Books, 1996) (Republished as **Ramadan Sonnets** by The Ecstatic Exchange 2005)
Long Days on Earth/Book VI (6-8/30/86)
Holograms (9/4/86 – 3/26/87)
History of the World (The Epic of Man's Survival) (4/7 – 6/18/87)
Exploratory Odes (6/25 – 10/18/87)
The Man at the End of the World (11/11 – 12/10/87)
The Perfect Orchestra (3/30 – 7/25/88)
Fed from Underground Springs (7/30 – 11/23/88)
Ideas of the Heart (11/27/88 – 5/5/89)
New Poems (scattered poems, out of series, from 3/24 – 8/9/89)

Facing Mecca (5/16 – 11/11/89)
A Maddening Disregard for the Passage of Time (11/17/89 – 5/20/90)
The Heart Falls in Love with Visions of Perfection (6/15/90 – 6/2/91)
Like When You Wave at a Train and the Train Hoots Back at You (Farid's Book) (6/11 – 7/26/91)
Orpheus Meets Morpheus (8/1/91 – 3/14/92)
The Puzzle (3/21/92 – 8/17/93)
The Greater Vehicle (10/17/93 – 4/30/94)
A Hundred Little 3-D Pictures (5/14/94 – 9/11/95)
The Angel Broadcast (9/29 – 12/17/95)
Mecca/Medina Time-Warp (12/19/95 – 1/6/96) (Published as a Zilzal Press chapbook, 1996)
Miracle Songs for the Millennium (1/20 – 10/16/96)
The Blind Beekeeper (11/15/96 – 5/30/97) (Published 2002 by Jusoor/Syracuse University Press)
Chants for the Beauty Feast (6/3 – 10/28/97)
Open Doors (10/29/97 – 5/23/98)
Salt Prayers (5/29 – 10/24/98) (Published by The Ecstatic Exchange, 2005)
Some (10/25/98 – 4/25/99)
Flight to Egypt (5/1 – 5/16/99)
I Imagine a Lion (5/21 – 11/15/99)
Millennial Prognostications (11/25/99 – 2/2/2000)
The Book of Infinite Beauty (2/4 – 10/8/2000)
Blood Songs (10/9/2000 – 4/3/2001)
The Music Space (4/10 – 9/16/2001)
Where Death Goes (9/20/2001 – 5/1/2002)
The Flame of Transformation Turns to Light (99 Ghazals Written in English) (5/2 – 6/29/2002)
Through Rose-Colored Glasses (7/22/2002 – 1/15/2003)
Psalms for the Broken-Hearted (1/22 – 5/25/2003) (Published by The Ecstatic Exchange, 2006)
Hoopoe's Argument (5/27 – 9/18/03)
Love is a Letter Burning in a High Wind (9/21 – 11/6/2003)
Laughing Buddha/Weeping Sufi (11/7/2003 – 1/10/2004) (Published by The Ecstatic Exchange, 2005)
Mars and Beyond (1/20 – 3/29/2004) (Published by The Ecstatic Exchange, 2005)
Underwater Galaxies (4/5 – 7/21/2004)
Cooked Oranges (7/23/2004 – 1/24/2005)
Holiday from the Perfect Crime (1/25 – 6/11/2005)
Stories Too Fiery to Sing Too Watery to Whisper (6/13 – 10/24/2005)
Coattails of the Saint (10/26/2005 – 5/10/2006)
In the Realm of Neither (5/14/2006 –)

www.ingramcontent.com/pod-product-compliance
Lightning Source LLC
Chambersburg PA
CBHW020920090426
42736CB00008B/715